# Animal Homes

Written by
Sarah Russell

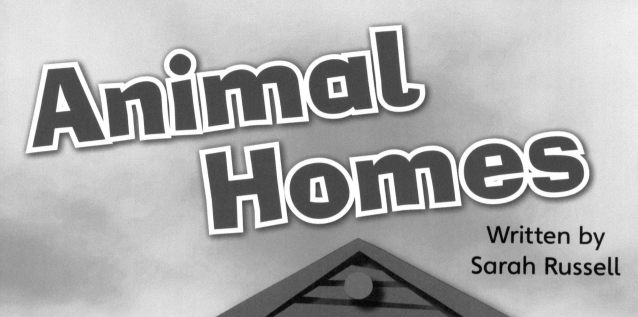

This is a duck's home.
A duck's home is a nest.

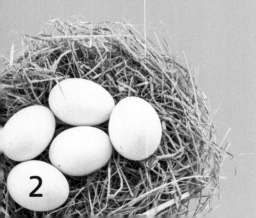

2

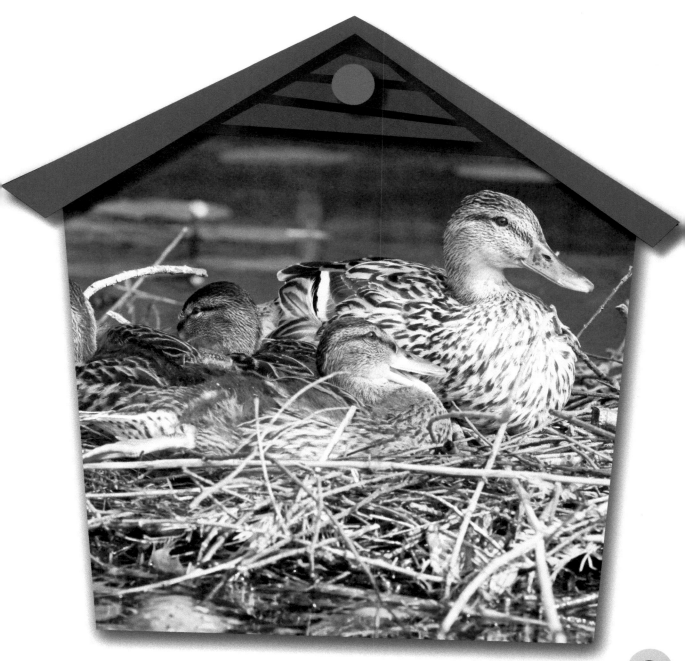

This is a bug's home.
A bug's home is a log.

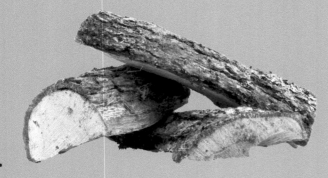

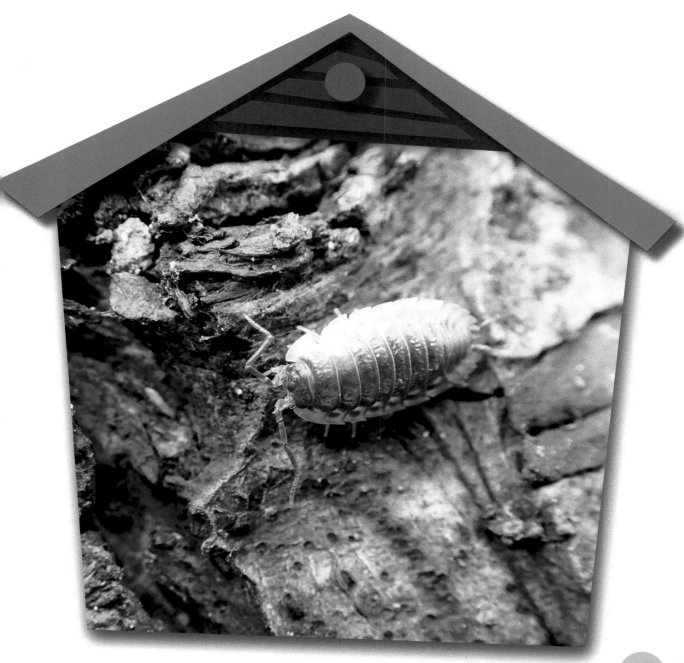

This is a rabbit's home.
A rabbit's home is a burrow.

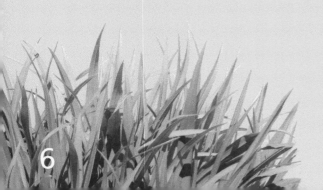

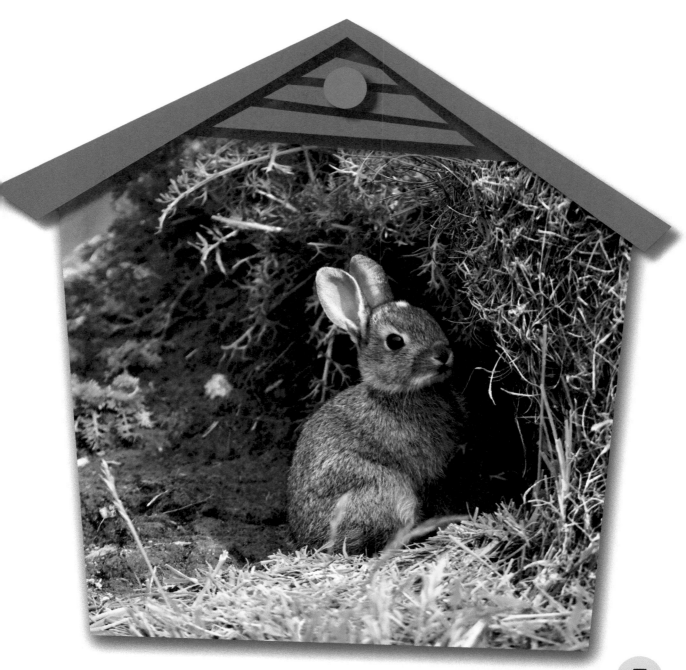

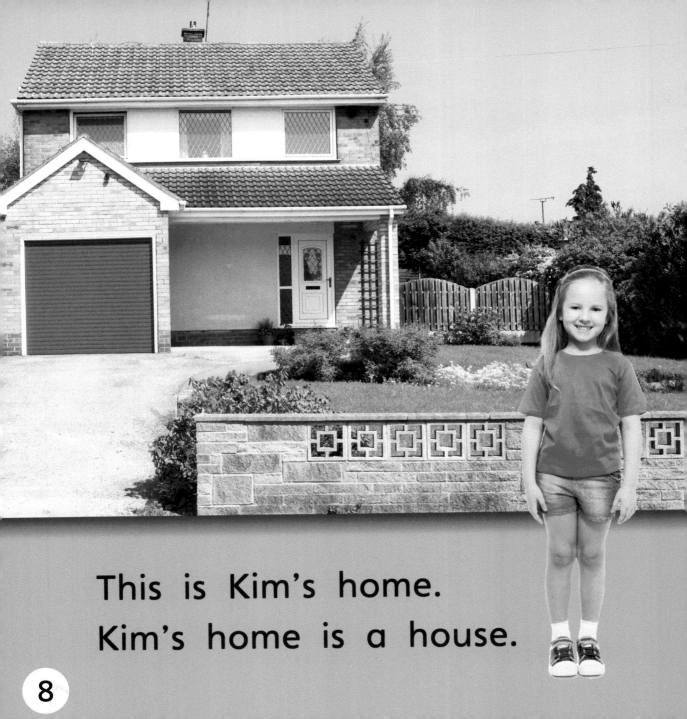

This is Kim's home.
Kim's home is a house.